Money, Credit and Inflation

An Historical Indictment of UK Monetary Policy and a Proposal for Change

GORDON PEPPER

With a Preface by
GEOFFREY E. WOOD
Professor of Economics,
City University Business School

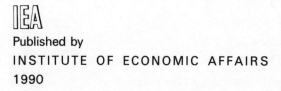

Published by
INSTITUTE OF ECONOMIC AFFAIRS
1990

First published in April 1990 by

The Institute of Economic Affairs,
2 Lord North Street,
Westminster, London SW1P 3LB

Research Monograph 44

ISSN 0073-9103
ISBN 0-255 36228-5

*The Institute gratefully acknowledges financial support for its
publications programme and other work from a generous benefaction
by the late Alec and Beryl Warren.*

Printed in Great Britain by
Goron Pro-Print Co. Ltd.,
Churchill Industrial Estate, Lancing, W. Sussex

Filmset in 'Berthold' Univers 9 on 11pt Medium

Contents

3

Foreword

The control of the money supply is a critical element in the management of the economy. In this *Research Monograph* Professor Gordon Pepper sets out the primary objective of monetary policy in unequivocal terms—to control inflation. As the British economy enters a new decade it has become apparent that even a government committed to sound money and monetary restraint has failed to curb inflation. This is a dismal conclusion given the significant changes which have taken place in the UK economy over the last decade. Despite the shock to the economy due to the devaluation of sterling following the abolition of exchange controls in 1979, and the rising unemployment, low inflation appears to have been a temporary respite, an elusive prize.

A number of explanations have been offered for the bout of inflation and the credit boom of the late 1980s. These include the Chancellor of the Exchequer's over-reaction to the Stock Market Crash of October 1987, his decision to shadow the deutschemark, and the tax cuts of the 1988 Budget which, many claimed, fuelled the consumer boom. The then Chancellor of the Exchequer, Nigel Lawson, responded to the critics by arguing that his policies were on course, and that he would re-double the fight against inflation in the face of what was no more and no less than a temporary 'blip'—the last word has now entered the business world's lexicon as a metaphor for any sustained adverse trend.

Professor Gordon Pepper's diagnosis of Britain's present economic difficulties does not turn on personalities or politics. He explains what went wrong in terms of an inherent weakness in the way the Bank of England seeks to control the money supply. Under the present system UK monetary authorities influence the money supply indirectly through demand-side intervention. The Bank of England uses interest-rate adjustments to choke off or increase the demand for money. However, if the Bank gets wrong the estimate of the interest rate necessary to reduce the demand for money then, as lender-of-last-resort, it must and does stand ready to supply the financial system with all the liquidity it demands. There is no attempt to restrain the banks' liquidity and therefore no effective means of controlling the supply of money.

Professor Pepper sees this as the basic weakness of the present system of intervention. He proposes that financial discipline should operate directly on the supply of money; that the Bank of England should limit the growth of its own balance sheet. In this way the Bank's ability to supply virtually unlimited liquidity to the financial system would be capped.

Professor Gordon Pepper is a recognised and respected expert on monetary and financial policy. His analysis and observations of the course of UK monetary policy are timely, and his proposals for reform provide yet another option requiring serious debate. He has, like several other IEA authors before, pointed to the flaws in current thinking and the institutions underpinning the British monetary system. Some IEA authors, such as Kevin Dowd in *Private Money*, propose radical reforms which would privatise the money supply. Others see the key to effective monetary policy in an independent Bank of England. These 'privatisation solutions' have found increasing support even within official circles. Still others see the practical solution in Europe, with early membership of the European Monetary System, and more ambitious schemes such as a European central bank and common currency. Professor Pepper offers a more modest administrative solution based on a detailed understanding of the operations of the Bank of England. But all these authors share the conviction that the institutional arrangements of the British monetary system are in need of an overhaul and are responsible for the monetary incontinence which permits inflationary pressures to erupt sporadically.

The IEA is an educational charity which does not express a corporate view nor endorse those of its authors. Its publications are dedicated to expanding knowledge about the nature of the economic system, and the ways in which markets and pricing mechanisms can be used to promote the welfare of consumers. Professor Pepper's factual analysis and proposals for reform will give policy-maker, politician and economics commentator alike cause to reflect on whether the present structure of UK monetary policy can be reformed to ensure that inflation is kept down and interest rates are allowed to reflect the real cost of capital.

April 1990   CENTO VELJANOVSKI

Preface

When the Conservative administration took office in 1979, one of its principal objectives was the reduction of inflation. In that it has succeeded. The underlying rate of inflation has been brought down from a peak of over 20 per cent in 1980 to a little over 6 per cent at the beginning of 1990. But simple comparison of these two figures conceals the limited extent of the Government's success.

First, its often-repeated objective is stable prices. Second, and of more immediate concern, the current rate of inflation is the result of an acceleration of inflation which has been going on since the beginning of 1988. Furthermore, the inflation figure *understates* the excess demand in the UK economy—for some of that excess has been satisfied from abroad. (There can be no doubt that a part of the trade deficit is highly desirable, resulting from the improved rate of return on capital in the UK making investment here more attractive. But not all the deficit can be thus accounted for; some portion is the result of excess demand.)

What has gone wrong? In his paper, Gordon Pepper starts from the premise that the problem was excessive money growth. Not everyone would accept this explanation. Some would maintain money is totally irrelevant to the inflationary process—this view was expressed most notably in the Radcliffe Report.[1] Others argue that inflation is largely a cost-push phenomenon, and that if monetary expansion did *not* accommodate these pressures the resulting squeeze would be felt primarily by real output. Monetary restraint would not restrain prices.

It is my opinion that the balance of evidence is clearly against these latter two views. Prolonged periods of slowly rising prices—such as Britain experienced from 1896 to 1913—are always accompanied by money growth slightly faster than income growth. Bouts of hyperinflation, such as China had from 1945 to 1949, are always associated with extraordinary surges in the rate of growth of money. This of course shows only association, *not* causation; it

---

[1] *The Working of the Monetary and Credit System* (Radcliffe Report), Cmnd. 827, London: HMSO, 1959.

could be consistent with the claim that prices were determined by non-monetary forces, and that had money risen more slowly only output would have been squeezed. But that is not the end of the evidence. If it is correct that slow money growth squeezes output, not prices, over a long period, then prolonged periods of slow money growth should be periods of sluggish performance in real terms. This is not the case. In Britain from 1873 to 1896 money grew more slowly than output. Yet real output growth then averaged no less than in the subsequent quarter-century, and prices fell. Similar facts can be set out for the United States, another country for which extensive historical data are available.

But even for those who reject such evidence, Gordon Pepper's paper is important. For the Government which took office in 1979 agreed that monetary control was necessary to control inflation. Nevertheless it failed to control money. Why? Was there a lack of will, or were the instruments of policy inadequate for the task? What produced the gap between intentions and achievement?

The last question is important for all concerned with economic policy, regardless of their views on the role of money in inflation.

Gordon Pepper's answer is that the tools were—and are— inadequate. The monetary base, M0, is a good indicator of inflationary pressure, but the present control procedure can correct only minor deviations from M0's desired path. In addition, the control of bank lending—also important for inflation, both directly through its influence on demand and indirectly through the effect of credit growth on the velocity and growth of M0—is, he argues, very weak.

The author's conclusion is that monetary control techniques must be reformed. He does in this paper make suggestions for that reform, but these are not his main theme. Nor does he examine why we have defective monetary control techniques after a decade of a government which thought monetary control important. What he has done in this fascinating *Research Monograph*, which is at once both vigorous and scholarly, is to re-open at the beginning of the 1990s the debate over monetary control that took place— ultimately to little effect—at the beginning of the 1980s.

It is time to consider how money can be controlled; for the control of money matters, and we are not doing it well enough.

February 1990

GEOFFREY WOOD
Professor of Economics,
City University Business School

The Author

GORDON T. PEPPER, CBE, is an Honorary Visiting Professor in the Department of Banking and Finance and Director of the Midland Montagu Centre for Financial Markets at the City University Business School. He is a member of the Economic and Social Research Council.

He is also a Director and Senior Adviser of Midland Montagu, which includes the stockbroking business of Greenwell Montagu. Gordon Pepper was previously Chairman of Greenwell Montagu & Co. and, prior to that, Joint Senior Partner of W. Greenwell & Co.

He was educated at Repton School and Trinity College, Cambridge, where he graduated in mathematics and economics.

In 1960 he was the joint founder of the gilt-edged business of W. Greenwell & Co. and revolutionised statistical techniques in the gilt-edged market and for many years was regarded as the leading commentator on the UK gilt-edged market. In 1972 he introduced W. Greenwell & Co.'s *Monetary Bulletin* which became one of the most widely read monetary economic publications produced in the United Kingdom.

He is a Fellow of the Institute of Actuaries and a Fellow of the Society of Investment Analysts.

For the IEA he has previously written: (with Geoffrey E. Wood) *Too Much Money . . .?* (Hobart Paper No. 68, 1976); *A firm foundation for monetary policy* (IEA Inquiry No. 8, 1989); and a short paper, 'Monetary Control, Past, Present and Future', in *The State of the Economy* (IEA Readings No. 31, 1990).

Acknowledgements

The author is in the debt of Roger Bootle, Alec Chrystal and Geoffrey Wood for helpful comments and discussion; any errors, of course, remain the author's.

December 1989   G.T.P.

ONE

Introduction

The underlying rate of inflation—that is, excluding changes in mortgage interest rates—has risen from 3·5 per cent in the year to February 1988 to 6·1 per cent in the year to January 1990. There has also been a huge deterioration in the current account of the balance of payments, some of which represents inflation in the pipeline that has yet to come out into the open.

The primary role of monetary policy is to control inflation. The fact is that UK monetary policy has clearly failed in its primary purpose.

Furthermore, the failure was glaring as the most important reason for the excessive monetary growth which the authorities allowed to occur was buoyancy of credit. If the reason had been a huge budget deficit, it could have been argued that fiscal policy was partly to blame. But, since the cause was borrowing by the private sector, the fault lies wholly with monetary policy.

The failure to stop inflation from rising was particularly disappointing given the Prime Minister's determination to prevent it. The failure was not one of political resolve but of technique of monetary control.

Remedial Action

Remedial action can be of two kinds. The first would be to change the domestic technique of monetary control to one which would be robust and reliable. The second would be to hand over responsibility for monetary policy to an external body that would be capable, i.e. to the Bundesbank.

The second option would mean the UK joining the Exchange Rate Mechanism (ERM) of the European Monetary System (EMS) and, further, following a policy of not 'sterilising' any foreign exchange outflow or inflow. Intervention in the foreign exchange market is said to be sterilised if its impact on the money supply is offset by official operations in the gilt-edged market. A policy of refraining from sterilisation would mean that intervention in the foreign exchange market to stop sterling from falling below its band would reduce the money supply—that is, monetary policy would automatically be tightened. The discipline would be similar to that of the pre-1914 Gold Standard.

Continuing with the European theme, competition between currencies has been put forward as an alternative to an early move to a common currency as proposed by the Delors Report. Sterling would have no chance of competing successfully against the deutschemark—the Bank of England would not have any hope in a contest with the Bundesbank—if the present system of monetary control remains. The Bank's only chance would be to go one better than the Bundesbank and adopt the control mechanism of the Swiss National Bank.

The conclusion is that even under competing currencies there is a need to change the domestic mechanism of monetary control to one which would be both robust and reliable: that is what this *Research Monograph* is about.

The Contents

Section 2 sets the background with a description of the inflationary pressures at the start of 1990.

Sections 3 to 8 describe the history of monetary policy in the 1980s. The objective of these sections is to clarify the record. What precisely were the signals coming from M0, the exchange rate and M4? What were the underlying causes of excessive monetary growth?

Sections 9 and 10 describe the present system of control, warts and all. Section 11 contains the details of the proposal to copy the Swiss National Bank—that is, that the Bank of England should control the growth of its own balance sheet. Section 12 starts with a brief history of the debate about the control mechanism in the UK before making some observations about a crucial issue. Section 13 makes some comments about the Exchange Rate Mechanism of the European Monetary System, i.e. about the alternative to a robust system of domestic control.

Section 14 contains the summary, followed by the policy conclusion in Section 15.

The best way to read the *Monograph* is probably to study first the list of the contents on pages 3-6, and then to turn straight to the summary of the main points, which starts on page 73. Some readers may have difficulty with the summary before they have read the relevant sections but a glance at it will give an idea of how the analysis proceeds. Some readers may wish to omit the discussion of Divisia Money and P-star Money in Section 6, as they are more technical than the rest of the paper. The same applies to the detail of money market operations in Section 11.

TWO

The Rise in Inflation

Chart I illustrates what has been happening to the UK's underlying rate of inflation. More precisely, the graph shows the annual rate of change of the Retail Price Index excluding the effect of changes in mortgage interest rates. The fall in inflation from over 20 per cent in 1980 to under 5 per cent in 1983 is clearly illustrated. The 'blip' from just over 4 per cent to over 5 per cent early in 1985 can also be seen. The current rise, which is giving such cause for concern, is from 3·5 per cent in February 1988 to 6·1 per cent in January 1990.

Chart II illustrates the dramatic deterioration in the current account of the UK's balance of payments, from rough balance in 1986 to a published deficit of over £20 billion in the year to September 1989. This chart has been included both as a measure of inflationary pressure not reflected in the published domestic rate of inflation and as an indication of inflation still in the pipeline.

The inclusion of Chart II is controversial. Firstly, it is highly likely that the published data for the balance of payments grossly exaggerate the size of the present current account deficit. The quality of the data is appalling; the *balancing item* in the balance of payments in the year to June 1989 was estimated in October 1989 to be £15 billion.

Secondly, capital can now flow freely across exchanges and is bound to flow from countries with lower than average rates of return on industrial investment to those with higher than average rates. It will, for example, flow from countries with persistent surplus domestic savings, perhaps because of demographic factors, to those with a chronic shortage. Such flows will affect exchange rates, which will then affect the current accounts of the balance of payments. Deficits on current account may, therefore, be part of a healthy process of economic adjustment and are not necessarily a cause for concern.

'An Unsustainable Consumer Boom'

The above two factors do not, however, account for the whole of the UK's current account deficit. A third factor is that the UK has

Chart I:
Underlying rate of inflation: UK, annual, 1979-89

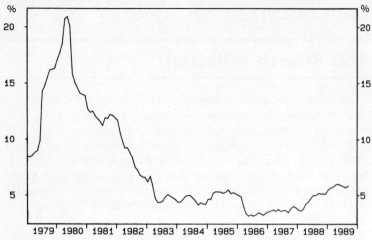

had an unsustainable consumer boom. This has sucked in imports and diverted exports to the home market. This part of the current account deficit is a symptom of inflationary pressure. As consumer expenditure reverts to a sustainable proportion of GDP, this part of the deficit will disappear.

Chart II:
Balance of payments, current account:
UK, monthly, 1979-89

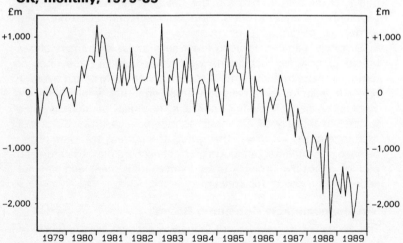

The final factor is more worrying. Chancellor Lawson used very high short-term interest rates to combat inflationary pressure. This encouraged an inflow of short-term capital, leading to an exchange rate higher than would otherwise have been the case. As the domestic inflationary pressure subsides, short-term interest rates will revert to a more normal level. Such a fall in interest rates is likely to lead to a decline in sterling, thereby raising external inflationary pressure. Domestic prices will, as a result, rise by more than would otherwise be the case. This is the inflation in the pipeline which has yet to pour out into the open.

THREE

The Story According to M0

For background perspective, Chart III shows the behaviour of M0 during the last decade. The solid line shows the rate of growth of M0 during 12-month periods and the dashed line shows the growth during six-month periods (annualised and seasonally adjusted). Points on the graphs are plotted at the end of the period to which they relate.

The Government started to target M0 in April 1984. Chart IV shows its behaviour since the beginning of that calendar year, together with the target ranges. The behaviour of base rates is also shown. This chart is designed to illustrate what was happening to interest rates when growth of M0 first became excessive. Six-month and three-month rates of growth (again annualised and seasonally adjusted) are shown because they are much more sensitive to a change in the trend of the series than are 12-month rates.

It will be seen that the three-month growth rates rose through the top of the target range for M0 on the following occasions:

July 1984	September 1986
November 1984	July 1987
December 1985	April 1988

On all of these occasions base rates rose, but not necessarily in the precise month. The reason why they did so may, or may not, be connected with the behaviour of M0 (see Section 4). The relevant point for the purpose of this Section is *that they were raised*, and the impact of this on M0 can be observed. The Appendix to this Section gives the precise data for M0 and the dates when base rates were raised on each occasion.

A. July 1984

The first incident was in July 1984. Base rates were raised from 9·25 per cent on 9 July to 12 per cent on 11 July. When this action was taken it was known that there had been a large (£109 million) rise in M0 in June but it was a month before publication of the rise in the three-month rate of growth above the top of the target range.

Chart III:
Growth rates of nominal M0: UK, 1979-89

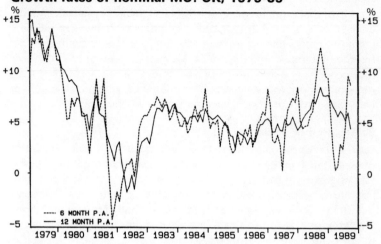

Chart IV:
Base rates and M0: UK, 1984-89

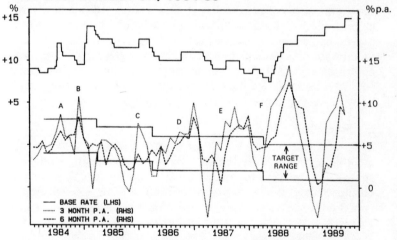

The combination of early action and the 2·75 per cent rise in base rates was sufficient to curtail the excessive monetary growth.

B. November 1984

Base rates were raised from 9·75 per cent on 11 January to 14 per cent on 28 January 1985. This action was taken one month after it was known that M0's three-month rate of growth to November had

19

exceeded the top of the target range. The excess monetary growth was larger than in July; the six-month rate of growth also exceeded the top of the target range. In spite of both the larger excess and the delayed action, the 4·25 per cent rise in base rates was more than enough to reduce the growth of M0. It was a clear case of overkill. By the autumn of 1985, M0's six-month rate of growth had dropped *below* the bottom of the target range, indicating that monetary policy would have been in danger of becoming too tight if base rates had not been lowered earlier in the year.

C. December 1985

Base rates were raised from 11·5 per cent to 12·5 per cent on 9 January 1986 in the month it became known that the three-month rate of growth of M0 had exceeded the top of the target range. The amount of excessive monetary growth was very small; the six-month rate of growth remained in the lower half of the target range. The prompt rise in base rates was sufficient corrective action; it might even have been unnecessary.

D. September 1986

Base rates were raised from 10 to 11 per cent on 14 October 1986 in the month it became known that M0's three-month rate of growth had started to exceed the top of the target range. M0's six-month rate of growth had also risen close to the top of the range and exceeded it the following month. In spite of the quite considerable excessive monetary growth and only a 1 per cent rise in base rates, this prompt action proved sufficient.

E. July 1987

Base rates rose from 9 to 10 per cent on 7 August 1987 in the month it became known that M0's three-month rate of growth had started to exceed the top of the target range. By early October the position looked similar to that at the end of 1986—considerable excess growth, only a 1 per cent rise in base rates but prompt early action. A major diversion then occurred.

First Major Diversion

On 19 October 1987 the stock market crashed worldwide. Base rates in the UK were reduced from 10 to 8·5 per cent by 4 December, at a time when the behaviour of M0 was indicating that the rise in rates in August had been insufficient. For control of M0 this was a major policy error. But, given the forecast deflationary impact of the stock-market crash, it was very understandable.

As a general rule, a central bank should give priority to lender-of-last-resort operations when a financial crisis occurs. When the crisis is over, the central bank should mop up the excess money injected into the banking system during the crisis. An interesting feature of the 1987 episode is the way in which the US Federal Reserve managed to revert to its earlier monetary policy and mop up the excess money but the UK authorities did not.

The relative success of the Federal Reserve is striking because the deflationary dangers were much greater in the USA than in the UK. First, the potential 'loss-of-wealth effect' was considerably larger because direct holding of shares by private individuals is much more important in the USA than in the UK. Second, US corporations' balance sheets were much weaker than those of UK corporations (suggesting that a recession might lead to financial difficulties which would then deepen the recession). Third, the crash in the world's stock markets originated in the USA.

It is interesting to note that by the middle of December 1987, prime rates in the US had fallen by only 0·5 per cent whereas UK base rates had been reduced by 1·5 per cent. (US prime rates did, however, fall by another 0·25 per cent early in February 1988, whereas UK base rates were *raised* by 0·5 per cent (on 2 February); US prime rates did not, in fact, start to rise until the second week of May 1988.)

Second Major Diversion

Base rates in the UK were reduced from 9 to 8·5 per cent on 17 March and to 8 per cent on 11 April, before falling to 7·5 per cent on 18 May 1988.

The monetary background was that M0's six-month rate of growth had been above the top of the target range for no less than the five months between the end of July and the end of December 1987. M0's growth then collapsed; it actually declined in both January and February 1988. This lowered the three-month rate of growth to 2·0 per cent by the end of March.

There is a strong argument that the authorities should not react quickly to a fall in monetary growth when it has been preceded by a period of considerable excess. This is because a period of sluggish growth is required to mop up the excess. If there has been no previous .excess it may be appropriate to react to a downturn quickly but, if there has been, it is usually most unwise to do so.

The unfortunate feature of the first few months of 1988 was that M0's downturn was consistent with the forecasts of recession following the stock-market crash. These forecasts suggested that

Table 1:
Change in MO: December 1987 to May 1988

	1-month £m.	3-month % p.a.	6-month % p.a.	12-month %
December 1987	135	7·4	8·4	4·3
January 1988	−42	3·4	5·2	4·6
February 1988	−13	2·0	4·4	5·3
March 1988	135	2·0	4·7	5·8
April 1988	112	6·1	4·7	6·1
May 1988	116	9·5	5·7	6·4

MO's deceleration would continue. This was a trap. In the event, MO rebounded. MO's exact behaviour is shown in Table 1.

The first indication of a rebound came with a £135 million rise in March 1988. The rebound then continued during the next two months. In the circumstances, the reductions in base rates from 8·5 to 8 per cent on 11 April and from 8 to 7·5 per cent on 18 May were completely inappropriate. The Chancellor had allowed himself to be diverted by his attempt to shadow the deutschemark.

F. April 1988

In spite of MO's three-month rate of growth once again exceeding the target range by April, base rates did not start to rise until 3 June 1988. By then, MO's 12-month rate of growth had exceeded the top of the target range by more than 1 per cent for two months. The initial decision to alter base rates in the wrong direction and the subsequent delay in taking corrective action allowed excessive growth of MO to gather momentum. The consequences for inflation were serious.

Assessment

Chancellor Lawson's first mistake was to think that MO was a leading rather than a nearly coincidental indicator of money GDP. With a leading indicator, the authorities have time to take corrective action but, if the indicator is merely coincidental, there is a danger that undesirable momentum will build up. His second mistake was to assume that he had an effective mechanism of control over MO. His speech to the Lombard Association in April 1986 provides a clear description of his thoughts at the time:

'The main point about this relationship between MO and money GDP is that M0 is a useful *advance* indicator: it is influenced by many of the factors that influence money GDP, especially changes in interest rates and disposable incomes, but these influences show up in M0 more immediately than they do in money GDP.

'And, in contrast to £M3, the growth of M0 responds fairly rapidly and predictably to changes in short-term interest rates. So a rise in interest rates can be expected to bring M0 growth back within its target range within a relatively short span of time.'

By the time of his October 1989 Mansion House speech, Mr Lawson had learnt differently, as shown by the following extract:

'M0 is for the most part a coincident indicator. This is very useful as it is many months before a reasonably reliable estimate of money GDP is available, but it does mean that M0 gives little early warning of inflationary pressures to come.'

If the Bank of England had been controlling the reserve base of the UK's banking system, the Chancellor would have been right to think that M0 was a leading indicator of money GDP. Causality would then have run from the quantity of bank reserves to the behaviour of money and credit and from there to money GDP. In practice, the Bank makes no attempt to control the quantity of bank reserves; it supplies whatever amount the banks want. With the Bank operating in this way, M0 very largely reflects the public's demand for notes and coin, which depends almost wholly on the level of retail sales. Under the current system, therefore, the data for M0 are best considered as a very up-to-date weekly proxy series for retail sales (in value rather than volume terms). M0 is a leading indicator of inflationary pressure, rather than being merely a coincidental indicator, only in the sense that unsustainable growth of retail sales for longer than six months or so will lead in due course to a balance-of-trade deficit, an overheated domestic economy, or both.

The second mistake was the assumption that there was an effective mechanism of control over M0. On the contrary, a rise in interest rates has very little direct impact on M0. The mechanism is the indirect one of an increase in interest rates affecting the economy in general and retail sales in particular. The slowdown in retail sales is then reflected in the behaviour of M0. This process can take some time to occur. Moreover, a rise in short-term interest rates may not have a powerful effect on the economy unless it is sufficiently large to constitute a definite shock.

Preliminary Conclusion

The conclusion at this stage is that, given the way in which the Bank operates and the possibly weak impact of interest rates on the economy, the mechanism of control was adequate to correct only minor departures of MO from its desired path. It was therefore essential that corrective action be taken promptly. Even so, it was most probably only a matter of time before a larger deviation occurred, possibly because the authorities had earlier guessed the wrong level of interest rates. When this happened, interest rates would have had to be raised very aggressively.

Chancellor Lawson's third mistake was that he allowed himself to be diverted by the October 1987 crash in the stock markets. He was unlucky that retail sales, and hence MO, happened to fluctuate downward in a way which was consistent with the forecasts of recession at the time. His mistake of paying too much attention to the stock-market crash is very easy to understand. But his mechanism of control was not sufficiently robust to allow for bad luck.

Mr Lawson's fourth mistake came on top of the others. He allowed himself to be diverted into attempting to shadow the deutschemark in the Spring of 1988. This was the crucial error. The cumulative effect of the four mistakes is the reason inflationary pressure has become so serious. This is the conclusion of the story from the point of view of MO.

Appendix to Section Three

A. July 1984 (4-8 per cent target range)

Change in MO

	1-month £m.	3-months % p.a.	6-months % p.a.
May	86	5·0	4·4
June	109	6·4	5·6
July	80	8·6*	6·6

Change in Base Rates

9 July: from 9·25 to 10%
11 July: from 10 to 12%

Assessment: Base rates rose when the £109 million increase in MO in June was known, but one month before it was known that the three-month rate of growth to July had exceeded the top of the target range.

Note: *signifies a rate of growth in excess of the target range for the fiscal year as a whole.

B. November 1984 (4-8 per cent target range)

Change in MO

	1-month £m.	3-months % p.a.	6-months % p.a.
September	106	5·8	6·1
October	16	3·8	6.2
November	226	10·7*	8·3*
December	−47	5·9	5·8

Change in Base Rates

11 January: from 9·75 to 10·5%
14 January: from 10·5 to 12%
28 January: from 12 to 14%

Assessment: Base rates rose one month after it was known that the three-month rate of growth to November had exceeded the top of the target range.

25

C. December 1985 (3-7 per cent target range)

Change in MO

	1-month £m.	3-months % p.a.	6-months % p.a.
November	74	1·6	2·3
December	186	7·6*	3·9

Change in Base Rates

9 January: from 11·5 to 12·5%

Assessment: Base rates rose in the month that it was known that the three-month rate of growth in MO had exceeded the top of the target range.

D. September 1986 (2-6 per cent target range)

Change in MO

	1-month £m.	3-months % p.a.	6-months % p.a.
August	129	5·2	4·9
September	85	6·5*	5·2
October	9	6·3*	6·1*
November	134	6·3*	5·7
December	215	10·0*	8·3*
January	−90	7·2*	6·7*

Change in Base Rates

14 October: from 10 to 11%

Assessment: Base rates rose in the month that it was known that the three-month rate of growth in MO had started to exceed the top of the target range.

E. July 1987 (2-6 per cent target range)

Change in MO

	1-month £m.	3-months % p.a.	6-months % p.a.
July	193	7·9*	4·1
August	42	7·1*	6·3*
September	114	9·5*	6·9*
October	106	7·0*	7·4*
November	39	6·9*	7·0*
December	135	7·4*	8·5*

Change in Base Rates

7 August: from 9 to 10%

Assessment: Base rates rose in the month that it was known that the three-month rate of growth in MO had started to exceed the top of the target range.

F. April 1988 (1-5 per cent target range)

Change in MO

	1-month £m.	3-months % p.a.	6-months % p.a.
March	135	2·0	4·7
April	112	6·1*	4·7
May	116	9·5*	5·7*
June	168	10·3*	6·1*
July	147	11·2*	8·6*
August	157	12·2*	10·9*
September+	256	14·5*	12·4*

+distorted upwards by a postal strike.

Change in Base Rates

3 June:	from 7·5 to 8%
6 June:	from 8 to 8·5%
22 June:	from 8·5 to 9%
29 June:	from 9 to 9·5%
5 July:	from 9·5 to 10%
19 July:	from 10 to 10·5%
8 August:	from 10·5 to 11%
25 August:	from 11 to 12%
25 November:	from 12 to 13%

Assessment: Base rates did not start to rise until one month after it was known that the three-month rate of growth in MO had started to exceed the top of its target range.

Source: Long runs of monetary data (1963-88), Bank of England, 1989; CSO, *Financial Statistics*, October 1989.

FOUR

The Story According to the Exchange Rate

Charts V and VI show the sterling/deutschemark exchange rate over the same periods as Charts III and IV. Chart VII shows the monthly underlying change in the UK's foreign exchange reserves during the period covered by Chart VI, i.e. during the more recent period. The points A, B, C, D, E and F which have been superimposed on Charts VI and VII correspond with those on Chart IV. The Appendix to this Section gives the data for base rates, exchange rates and foreign exchange reserves on each occasion.

Summer 1984

Point A (in Chart VI) in the Summer of 1984 illustrates a fairly typical pattern. Sterling had been weak for some months. The exchange rate had been falling despite deployment of the reserves. More precisely, the rate had fallen from DM 3·97 on 27 January to DM 3·71 on 9 July, in spite of support for sterling of $188 million in March, $155m. in April, $128m. in May and $135m. in June. The weakness then escalated early in July. As the foreign exchange intervention was not producing the desired result, the authorities brought the interest-rate weapon into play. The escalation of the pressure early in July can be seen from the fact that the reserves declined by £268 million although base rates rose fom 9·25 to 12 per cent half way through the month.

Winter 1984-85

The story at Point B (in Chart VI) in the Winter of 1984-85 is also one of escalation following persistent weakness. On this occasion the decline in the exchange rate during the preliminary period was more marked. The reserves had not, however, fallen, indicating that the authorities had not been intervening to support sterling. Sterling's weakness then escalated. The rate declined quite sharply in spite of substantial use of the reserves ($282 million during January 1985) and the interest-rate weapon was again used.

Chart V:
Sterling/Deutschemark exchange rate: weekly, 1979-89

Chart VI:
Sterling/Deutschemark exchange rate: daily, 1984-89

Winter 1985-86

During the run up to Point C in the Winter of 1985-86, the reserves had been falling for some months and the exchange rate had been declining quite sharply. The escalation of the pressure on sterling before the rise in base rates can be seen from the sharp decline in the exchange rate, shown in Chart VI, and from the $416 million loss of reserves in December 1985 (Chart VII).

Chart VII:
Underlying change in official reserves: monthly, 1984-89

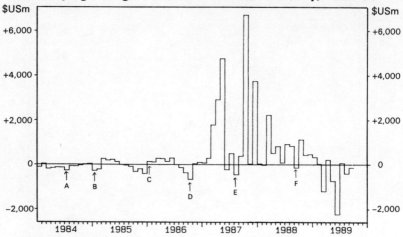

Autumn 1986

The description of Point D in the Autumn of 1986 is complicated by falling oil prices. The price of oil fell from $30 a barrel in November 1985 to $10 a barrel in July 1986. This was a 'real' factor, affecting the UK's balance of trade on oil account, to which the economy would have to adjust. Following the rise in base rates in January 1986, sterling had fallen to just below DM 3·40. Apart from one bout of weakness the currency then became quite firm and the authorities intervened until the end of June to stop the exchange rate from rising. Early in July sterling weakened sharply. The rate fell rapidly in spite of progressively greater use of the reserves ($4 million in July, $141 million in August and $372 million in September). The escalation of pressure is indicated by the $668 million loss of reserves in October. Base rates were raised by 1 per cent on 11 October.

Recapitulation

The story so far is basically the same on each occasion—persistent weakness, followed by a sudden deterioration, of sterling. The behaviour of sterling was the factor determining the timing of increases in base rates. Importantly, however, on every occasion the behaviour of M0 was also giving cause for concern, as described in Section 3. The two indicators of the stance of monetary policy gave the same message on each occasion. Of the two, the exchange rate was what broke the decision-taking inertia.

30

The Louvre Accord and Pegging Sterling

The story starts to change with the Louvre Accord in February 1987, when the leading central bankers of the world agreed to provide support for a weak dollar. The UK intervened massively in the following three months. Our foreign exchange reserves rose by the huge amounts of $1,785 million in March, $2,912 million in April and $4,760 million in May 1987, as illustrated very clearly in Chart VII.

The exchange-rate graph, Chart VI, adds very important detail. Intervention under the Louvre Accord concealed a policy of pegging sterling to the deutschemark. The size of the intervention was precisely the amount needed to peg sterling's exchange rate against the deutschemark to just below 3·0. A policy agreed for one purpose was used for another. This was the background to the run up to Point E in the Summer of 1987.

Summer 1987

The decision to raise base rates by 1 per cent was taken on 7 August 1987. It was not prompted by a decline in the exchange rate but by the amount of intervention required to maintain sterling at its pegged rate. Following the huge $4,760 million increase in May, the reserves had fallen by $230 million in June and had then risen by $499 million in July. The fall of $457 million in August, which occurred in spite of the rise in base rates towards the beginning of the month, is an indication of the foreign exchange pressure. At Point E, the exchange rate and M0 were basically telling the same story but the message from M0 was by far the clearer.

In October 1987 sterling again became extremely firm. The rate against the deutschemark was held at almost exactly 3·0 through-out the month. In order to peg it, the Bank of England intervened during the month by the incredible amount of $6,699 million. This pegging of the exchange rate at DM 3·0 continued until 4 March 1988. The movements in the reserves were +$31 million in November, +$3,737 million in December, +$38 million in January and –$25 million in February. In March sterling once again became very firm, and this firmness continued until the end of May. The reserves rose by $2,225 million in March, $514 million in April and $814 million in May. This time, however, the rate was not pegged. As the exchange rate rose to DM 3·2, base rates were reduced, from 11 to 10·5 per cent on 10 March, to 10 per cent on 19 March, to 9·5 per cent on 29 April, and to 9 per cent on 11 May. During this period the Treasury argued that the strength of sterling was an indication that monetary policy was tight and, further, that the inflationary effect of every 0·5 per cent reduction in base rates was being offset by each 2 per cent rise in the exchange rate.

Summer 1988

Sterling eventually reached a local peak of DM 3·19 on 27 May 1988. The first increase in base rates came on 3 June when sterling had fallen to DM 3·10.

Conclusion

The exchange rate was a good indicator of the mild inflationary pressure which materialised from time to time before the end of 1986. In the Summer of 1987 its signal became weak. The indicator then broke down completely. In the Spring of 1988 there was a clear message of re-assurance which was completely false at a most inopportune time. The danger light from the exchange rate did not start flashing until June 1988. It flashed again in September 1988 but it did not shine really brilliantly until March 1989.

Appendix to Section Four

A. Summer 1984

Base Rates:

10 May 1984:	from 8·5 to 9%
27 June:	from 9 to 9·25%
9 July:	from 9·25 to 10%
11 July:	from 10 to 12%

£/DM exchange rate:

27 January 1984:	3·97
4 June:	3·73
27 June:	3·77
9 July:	3·71

Change in underlying reserves ($m.):

March 1984	−188
April	−155
May	−128
June	−135
July	−268

B. Winter 1984-85

Base Rates:

11 January 1985:	from 9·75 to 10·5%
14 January:	from 10·5 to 12%
28 January:	from 12 to 14%

£/DM exchange rate:

13 September 1984:	3·86
11 January 1985:	3·56

Change in underlying reserves ($m.):

November 1984	12
December	36
January 1985	−282

C. Winter 1985-86

Base Rates:

9 January 1986:	from 11·5 to 12·5%

£/DM exchange rate:

10 July 1985:	4·07
7 January 1986:	3·51

Change in underlying reserves ($m.):

July 1985	−9
August	−36
September	−97
October	−324
November	−201
December	−416
January 1986	+132

D. Autumn 1986

Base Rates:

14 October 1986:	from 10 to 11%

£/DM exchange rate:

2 April 1986:	3·49
1 July:	3·37
14 October:	2·84

Change in underlying reserves ($m.):

July 1986	−4
August	−141
September	−372
October	−668
November	+35

Note: The price of oil fell from $30 a barrel in November 1985 to $10 a barrel in July 1986.

E. Summer 1987

Base Rates:

7 August 1987:	from 9 to 10%

£/DM exchange rate:

11 March 1987:	2·98
16 July:	3·00
7 August:	2·96

Change in underlying reserves ($m.):

May 1987	4,760
June	−230
July	499
August	−457

F. Spring/Summer 1988

Base Rates:

3 June 1988:	from 7·5 to 8%
6 June:	from 8 to 8·5%
22 June:	from 8·5 to 9%
29 June:	from 9 to 9·5%
5 July:	from 9·5 to 10%
19 July:	from 10 to 10·5%
8 August:	from 10·5 to 11%
25 August:	from 11 to 12%
25 November:	from 12 to 13%

£/DM exchange rate:

27 May 1988:	3·19
3 June:	3·10
6 June:	3·10
22 June:	3·15
29 June:	3·12
5 July:	3·11

Change in underlying reserves ($m.):

March 1988	2,225
April	514
May	814
June	84
July	910
August	827
September	−143

Source: CSO, *Financial Statistics*, October 1989; Supplementary data from Bank of England and Midland Montagu.

FIVE

The Record of Broad Money

Broad money was a superb indicator of inflationary pressure in the early 1970s. In complete contrast, it was a hopeless indicator of recessionary pressure in 1980-81.

An important reason for the contrast was distortions caused by the mechanism of monetary control and changes to it. In the early 1970s every one of the various measures of broad money was distorted upwards by 'round-tripping' transactions. These occurred because base rates tended at the time to lag behind money market rates and this gave people the opportunity to borrow from their bank when interest rates were rising in order to place the money on deposit, or purchase a certificate of deposit (CD), for a guaranteed profit. Both bank lending and deposits were artificially inflated as a result. This upward distortion to bank deposits amplified an underlying acceleration in £M3 in the early 1970s and made M3 a dramatic indicator of the inflation which was to come.

Distortions to £M3[1]

The distortion to £M3 in 1980-81 was also upward but on this occasion the distortion tended to mask an underlying deceleration. This spoilt, rather than accentuated, £M3's performance as an indicator. There were three types of distortion:

(i)   Banks competed aggressively with building societies to regain market share. As a result bank deposits, rather than building society deposits, rose.

(ii) In the late 1970s banks had been penalised if their interest-bearing-eligible-liabilities grew faster than a rate set by the Bank of England. This 'corset' control was abolished in the middle of 1980. Whilst it was in place, a bank could circumvent the control by persuading some customers to issue a commercial bill rather than take a loan and other customers to purchase a commercial bill rather than buy a CD. Whilst such

---

[1] £M3 was first published in March 1977: M3 included foreign currency deposits; £M3 did not.

Chart VIII:
Growth rates of nominal M3: UK, 1979-89

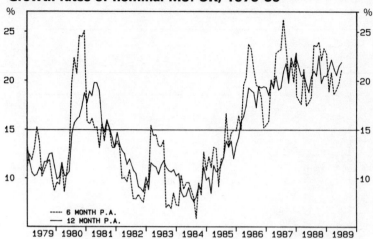

bill arbitrage was taking place £M3 was distorted downwards. After the corset was abolished, the transactions unwound and £M3 was distorted upwards.

(iii) The corset could also be circumvented if banking business was diverted overseas to the euro-sterling market. After the corset was abolished, £M3's growth was distorted upwards as euro-sterling deposits returned home.

The discussion of the three distortions has concentrated on the effect on £M3. Some of them affected the even broader definitions of the money supply and some did not. The broader series were changed in 1987. The old ones had been designated PSL1 and PSL2; the new ones were called M4 and M5. Simplifying, PSL1 had consisted of £M3 (i.e. notes and coin and sterling bank deposits) plus bills. PSL2 had consisted of PSL1 plus building society deposits. The second of the above distortions did not affect PSL1 and neither the first nor the second affected PSL2. Of the new series, £M3 was renamed M3 (and M3 became M3C), while M4 was defined to be M3 plus building society deposits. M5 was defined to be M4 plus bills—that is, it is similar to the old PSL2. The first of the above distortions would not have affected the data for M4, and neither the first nor the second would have affected those for M5.

Charts VIII, IX and X show the behaviour of M3, M4 and M5 since 1979. In all three charts, the solid graph lines show the rates of

Chart IX:
Growth rates of nominal M4: UK, 1979-89

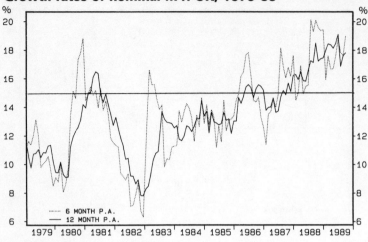

Chart X:
Growth rates of nominal M5: UK, 1979-89

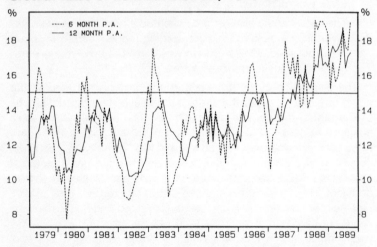

growth during 12-month periods and the dashed ones show the growth over six months (annualised and seasonally adjusted). (The official series for M4 is available only from the middle of 1982; prior to then, Chart IX shows the growth of M3 plus PSL2 less PSL1.)

If the three charts are compared it will be seen that the patterns in the late 1970s and early 1980s are consistent with the above description of the distortions:

o The build-up of inflationary pressure in 1978-79 was reflected best in M5. Downward distortion because of the 'corset' was the explanation for the relatively poor performance of M3 and M4 as indicators.

o M3 was by far the worst of the three indicators, erroneously warning of a renewed bout of inflation in 1980. M4 was also badly distorted by the ending of the corset. Although M5 was not distorted so badly, it was still very misleading.

M5 and M0 in 1980

Table 2 compares the behaviour of M5 with that of M0 in the middle and at the end of 1980. It will be seen that in May 1980 M0's growth was just below that of M5. By the end of the year the gap had become much larger—M0's growth had fallen whilst M5's had risen. M0 was correctly reflecting the recessionary pressure which existed at the time;[1] M5 was not. An explanation for M5's behaviour was the return of euro-sterling deposits, following the ending of the corset,[2] but it is very doubtful whether it was a sufficient one. (Anyone arguing that the explanation was a sufficient one should be careful about consistency with the early 1970s when the distortions were probably even greater; if they

Table 2:
Behaviour of the Money Supply:
M0 and M5 Compared, May and December 1980

	M0	M5	Difference
		per cent p.a.	
May 1980			
six-month growth	7·4	9·3	1·9
12-month growth	9·4	10·6	1·2
December 1980			
six-month growth	4·1	15·8	11·7
12-month growth	4·6	13·1	8·5

[1] See Alan Walters, *Britain's Economic Renaissance*, Oxford: Oxford University Press, 1986.

[2] See Tim Congdon, *Monetarism Lost*, London: Centre for Policy Studies, 1989.

Chart XI:
Growth rates of real M4: UK, 1979-89

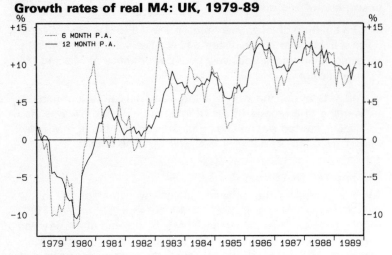

were sufficiently large in 1980 to turn broad money from an expansionary into a contractionary indicator, they would most probably have done the same during the earlier period—that is, they would have spoilt broad money's performance as an indicator of the awful inflation of the 1970s.)

Growth of M4 in the 1980s

Turning to more recent years, the behaviour of M3 should be disregarded because building societies have become progressively more like banks as they have introduced cheque books, cash machines, etc. It will be seen from the graphs that the behaviour of M4 and M5 has been very similar, because there have not been any major distortions to the system that have caused bill arbitrage similar to 1979-80. Attention can, therefore, be focussed on M4.

A detailed examination of the recent behaviour of M4 cannot be carried out in the same way as that for M0 in Section 3. M0's behaviour was assessed relative to its target range. M4 has not, in contrast, been targeted. The targets for broad money during the earlier years were set for £M3 rather than M4 and they were shifted before being scrapped in 1987. It is better, therefore, to assess the growth of M4 relative to inflation. Chart XI shows M4's growth in real terms.

It will be seen that the graph lines in Chart XI are well above the zero line since the end of 1982—M4's rate of growth has been

40

substantially greater than inflation. Since 1982 M4's behaviour has persistently been giving cause for concern, apart from a brief period of reassurance early in 1985 when there was a dip in the six-month rate of growth (the dashed graph line). The warnings of rising inflation from M4 came much too soon. It became discredited as an indicator.

Assessment

Because of the recent burst in inflation, M4 has become a fashionable indicator once again. The record of the first half of the 1980s, however, illustrates the way in which it can be very unreliable if it is used on its own. The next section starts with a discussion of how M4 should be supported by other information.

SIX

More Complex Assessments

Savings Money and Relative Interest Rates

Broad money is held either for transactions or for savings purposes. The latter can be either temporary or long term. Changes in the merits of a bank deposit as a medium for long-term savings have been an important reason for the wide variations in the efficiency of broad money as an indicator of inflationary pressure during the last two decades.

In the early 1970s bank deposits were a most unattractive home for genuine savings. There were two basic reasons for this. The first concerned the term structure of interest rates; the pattern was that interest rates tended to rise quite sharply as the term of an investment increased (i.e., the yield curve had a steep upward slope). The second reason was that interest rates tended to be negative in real terms. As a result of these two factors, the rate of interest on a bank deposit tended to be both below the rate of inflation and lower than the return on most other investments. This discouraged savers.

The opposite conditions occurred during the first three-quarters of 1980. The rate of interest on a bank deposit was well above the rate of inflation and the yield curve was inverted—that is, the income from a bank deposit was amongst the highest available in the market. In complete contrast to the 1970s, bank deposits were a most attractive home for genuine savings. Another factor in 1980 was that people became wary as the economy slid into recession. They started to spend less and save more. With the precautionary motive for savings high, the liquidity and capital certainty attributes of a bank deposit were further attractions to savers.

Following the above reasoning, there was a strong argument in 1980 that the underlying buoyancy of broad money at the time was a reflection of an increase in savings, i.e. that it was a symptom of the decline in economic activity which was occurring rather than of inflationary pressure. As long as the yield curve remained inverted, there was a strong case for focussing attention on the narrow definitions of money, including M0.[1]

---

[1] See 'Alarm Bells', *Monetary Bulletin* No. 193, London: Midland Montagu, August 1987.

Divisia Money

A formal method of dividing broad money into that held for transactions and that held for savings purposes is the 'Divisia' approach.[1] Under this method, the forms of money which earn no interest are deemed to be pure transactions money. Notes and coin and non-interest-bearing bank deposits are, accordingly, classified solely as transactions money. At the other extreme, the forms of money which earn the full market rate of interest are deemed to be pure savings money—for example, certificates of deposit. In between, the other categories of money are apportioned between transactions and savings depending on the ratio of the rate of interest payable on the category relative to the full market rate of interest.

The historical series[2] which have been derived for Divisia money in the UK perform well as an indicator of inflation throughout the 1970s and during the 1980s up to the time of writing (December 1989). At first sight, the concept looks very encouraging. But further examination suggests that, whereas it may be of considerable use for historical analysis, it is of little practical use as a tool for assessing very recent monetary conditions. The reason for being suspicious of its reliability comes from an examination of the way in which the weights for the components in the Divisia calculation vary. Very briefly, building society deposits comprise about 40 per cent of M4. The weights for these deposits vary drastically as building society rates lag behind movements in money market rates. The combination of the size of the component and the variation in weight can easily dominate the short-run behaviour of Divisia M4. A deceleration of Divisia M4 often merely reflects that interest rates have risen recently.

P-star Money

The concept behind P-star money is relatively simple. It relates the equilibrium level of the money supply to the equilibrium level of prices. If the current level of the money supply is in excess of that 'compatible' with the current price level, inflation will rise. The starting point to this approach is the quantity theory of money:

---

[1] W. Barnett, E. Offenbacher, P. Spindt, 'New Concepts of Aggregated Money', *Journal of Finance*, May 1981.

[2] R. A. Batchelor, 'The Monetary Services Index', *Economic Affairs*, June/July 1988; M. T. Belongia, K. A. Chrystal, 'An Admissible Monetary Aggregate for the United Kingdom', Federal Reserve Bank of St. Louis Working Paper, revised November 1989; P. D. Spencer, 'Monetary Policy in the 1980's: A New Monthly Measure of the UK Money Supply', London: Shearson Lehman Hutton, February 1989.

$$MV = PQ$$

where   M is the money stock

V is the velocity of circulation

P is the price level

and   Q is the quantity of output.

In most economies, the quantity of output, i.e. real GDP, has a reasonably clear underlying trend over time. Let the trend output at the current point of time be Q*. The velocity of circulation also has an underlying trend. Let the current trend velocity be V*. Then P* is defined as:

$$P^* = \frac{MV^*}{Q^*}$$

P* is the equilibrium price level given the current level of the money stock. If P* is above the current level of prices, P, inflation will rise. If P* is below P, inflation will fall.

The main practical value of the P-star approach is that it focusses attention on the amount of excess money currently in the economy as well as on the current rate of growth of the money supply. In the USA, the concept has been applied mainly to the M2 definition of money.[1] In the UK, it has been suggested that the approach should be applied to M0.[2]

It was argued in Section 3 that, given the way the Bank of England operates in practice, M0 is demand rather than supply determined. Under the present UK system there cannot be an excess supply of M0 in the sense that it is larger than people's demand for notes and coin, but there can be an excess supply relative to the availability of goods and services. The growth of M0 in the UK is little more than a proxy for the growth of retail sales. The stock of M0 is a proxy for the level of retail sales. The P-star approach applied to M0 in the UK would focus attention on the level of retail sales as well as on its rate of growth. If inflation is to be avoided, the level of retail sales (and of consumer expenditure) must be a satisfactory proportion of GDP (in the sense that it allows

---

[1] J. J. Hallman, R. D. Porter, D. H. Small, *M2 per Unit of Potential GNP as an Anchor for the Price Level*, Federal Reserve Board of Governors, April 1989.

[2] S. Hannah, A. James, *P-Star as a Monetary Indicator for the UK*, NatWest Capital Markets, June 1989.

room for a level of investment consistent with the underlying trend of output).

The historical series which have been derived for the ratio of P*M0 to P in the UK look promising as an indicator of inflation. The exact level of P*M0 relative to P is, however, sensitive to the assumptions made about the trends in the velocity of circulation and in output. There is, accordingly, a considerable margin of doubt about exactly when P*M0 is equal to P. This conclusion suggests that the P-star approach is useful but that it should not be followed slavishly.

SEVEN

Causes of Monetary Growth

If the Bank of England controlled the quantity of reserves in the UK banking system, causality would run from bank reserves to money and credit and from there to GDP. The starting point of analysis would then be the behaviour of bank reserves. The fact is, however, that the Bank does not behave in this way. The Bank supplies whatever quantity of reserves the banks want, and it is very important, therefore, to start analysis one stage further back and ascertain the reasons the money supply is behaving as it is.

The explanation of the buoyant growth of M0 in 1988 was increased demand for notes and coin because of a boom in retail sales. Much of the boom was financed by personal borrowing. In this sense the boom in credit was a cause of growth in M0.

In order to avoid confusion it should be emphasised that inflation is a monetary, not a credit, phenomenon. If there is a boom in bank lending, the important feature is not the provision of credit but the consequence for the money supply of credit being provided in the particular way.

The reasons for the behaviour of the money supply can be appreciated more fully by examining the counterparts of M4. The growth of M4 is directly influenced by:

o Fiscal policy: The Public Sector Borrowing Requirement (PSBR).

o Foreign exchange policy: The rise in the UK's foreign exchange reserves, less foreign financing of the public sector.

o Debt policy: Sales of public sector debt to the UK private sector (other than to banks or building societies).

o Credit policy: Sterling lending to the UK private sector by banks and building societies.

Table 3 gives the data for *annual* periods during the last few years.

Table 3:
Counterparts of M4: December 1985 to June 1989

(£000 million)

Year Ending	Fiscal Policy†	Foreign Exchange Policy	Debt Policy	Credit Policy	Other*	Growth of M4
Dec-85	7·5	−3·1	−8·1	34·0	−4·4	*25·9*
Mar-86	5·7	−1·8	−4·2	34·9	−4·6	29·9
Jun-86	5·4	−1·4	−3·2	37·4	−4·8	33·4
Sep-86	6·1	−2·0	−4·4	40·7	−5·9	34·5
Dec-86	2·4	−2·0	−5·9	47·1	−6·8	*34·7*
Mar-87	3·4	−1·7	−5·2	46·7	−10·1	33·1
Jun-87	2·4	1·6	−6·8	49·3	−12·3	34·2
Sep-87	−0·7	0·5	−2·9	53·4	−12·6	37·8
Dec-87	−1·5	7·2	−4·0	53·3	−12·6	*42·5*
Mar-88	−3·5	7·5	−5·4	60·8	−14·1	45·3
Jun-88	−6·4	4·7	−2·2	69·6	−18·5	47·2
Sep-88	−8·9	8·1	−2·3	77·2	−19·6	54·5
Dec-88	−11·5	3·3	3·7	82·0	−24·1	*53·4*
Mar-89	−14·3	2·2	9·8	85·4	−26·1	57·0
Jun-89	−12·9	1·0	12·5	83·8	−23·6	60·8

* Growth of non-deposit sterling liabilities of banks and building societies *less* their external and foreign currency transactions.

† A minus sum equals a PSDR (Public Sector Debt Repayment).

Source: CSO, *Financial Statistics.*

The following features will be noted:

Credit Policy

Credit was the overwhelming driving force behind M4's buoyancy. It rose from £34·0 billion in the calendar year 1985 to no less than £83·8 billion in the year to June 1989.

Fiscal Policy

The change in fiscal policy over the years was a very important offsetting factor; it was definitely *not* a cause of M4's buoyant growth. In the calendar year 1985 the public sector had a borrowing requirement of £7·5 billion. In the year to June 1989, the public sector had a debt repayment of £12·9 billion. Even if the stance of fiscal policy in 1988-89 is assessed by the £4·3 billion cut in taxation in the 1988 Budget, the direct impact of this reduction was small compared with that of credit. This is not to deny that there was an indirect effect; the tax cuts had an important impact on confidence and, therefore, on people's willingness to borrow.

Foreign Exchange Policy

The expansionary effect on M4 of the policy of resisting a rise in sterling is highlighted by the figures of £7·2 billion in the calendar year 1987 and £8·1 billion in the year to September 1988. Taking the latter first, it will also be seen that there was a public sector debt repayment (PSDR) of £8·9 billion in the year to September 1988. Nevertheless, debt was not repurchased; £2·3 billion was sold during the period. The debt sales were, in fact, £3·2 billion larger than the total required to cover the combination of the PSDR and the rise in the UK's foreign exchange reserves. In technical jargon, the authorities more than 'sterilised' the foreign exchange intervention.

Experience in the calendar year 1987 was slightly different. The authorities did not sterilise the intervention completely within the year but they managed to do so, and with a margin to spare, during the following quarter.

The conclusion is that the direct impact of foreign exchange policy on M4 was of minor importance. Again, this is not to deny that there was an indirect effect. As explained in Section 4, the authorities' reluctance to allow sterling to appreciate was a reason why interest rates were reduced. Even so, the main role of foreign exchange policy was diversionary rather than causal, as argued in that section.

Debt Policy

It is clear from Table 3 that debt policy was not a cause of M4's buoyancy. It was a weapon which could have been used to combat buoyant monetary growth. In 1985 the earlier policy of selling debt in specific quantities to control £M3 (overfunding) had been suspended because it was having very bad side-effects (in particular, the term structure of short rates had become completely dominated by the Bank having to roll over its consequentially huge mountain of commercial bills). Nevertheless, aggressive sales of debt during short periods from time to time would not necessarily have been inconsistent with the new policy of not generally overfunding. The authorities, however, chose not to deploy this weapon.

EIGHT

Asset Price Inflation

As already described, the buoyancy of broad money and credit in the 1980s was similar to that in the 1970s, but the early results were very different. In the 1970s the main outcome was an appalling rise in inflation, more precisely in product price inflation. In the 1980s an important initial outcome was a rise in the stock market and in the value of property—that is, in asset price inflation.

It was argued in Section 6 that bank deposits were an excellent home for genuine savings in 1980, when the rate of interest on them was high relative to both inflation and longer-term investments. In 1981 short-term interest rates fell and the income from a bank deposit was no longer the highest available in the market. Furthermore, a bull market started on the stock exchange. Holders of bank deposits observed other investors enjoying capital profits on bonds and stocks. Some of them switched out of bank deposits into these securities, expecting them to be a better investment. These transactions encouraged the bull market which usually occurs during the recovery stage of the business cycle.

The purchase of securities did not destroy the bank deposits. A purchase cannot be executed without there being a sale. The seller becomes the owner of the purchaser's bank deposit. The re-investment of some of these deposits in other securities provided another fillip to the bull market.

Bull Market Boosted—Again

People also started to borrow to make additional purchases of securities, as the bull market generated expectations of further capital profits. The sellers then received the bank deposits which were the counterpart of the buyers' loans. Re-investment of these deposits in other securities gave the bull market yet another boost.

The bull market spread from the stock market to property, in particular to houses. The rise in equity prices lasted from the autumn of 1981 until October 1987, when the US stock market crashed. House prices rose rapidly in real terms from the beginning of 1982 until the Summer of 1988.

The rise in asset prices was an important cause of the consumer

49

boom in 1987 and 1988. People became more wealthy. Some spent a portion of their capital gains. They were able to do so because other people borrowed to acquire the assets from them. There was also direct borrowing to finance consumption. People's confidence had risen and this made them more willing to borrow rather than wait until expenditure could be financed out of income in the future. Dissaving increased. With the rise in wealth, saving out of income also declined as people had less incentive to add to their wealth. Such declines in gross saving and rises in dissaving were important explanations why net savings, as measured by the personal savings ratio, fell from 9·4 per cent in 1985 to 4·4 per cent in 1988.

In 1987 and 1988 the Government appeared not to be perturbed by the asset price inflation which was occurring. It was interpreted as a measure of people's increased confidence in the Government, and this of course the politicians enjoyed. The argument that it was a form of inflation driven by excessive growth of money and credit was dismissed in a way that was all too similar to the dismissal of the monetarist arguments in the early 1970s.

Summary

This section can be summarised as follows. Buoyant growth of broad money and credit in the 1980s led at first to asset price inflation. This contributed to the subsequent buoyancy of consumer demand and then fed through to product price inflation. Inflation followed the excessive growth of broad money but the time-lag between the excessive growth and product price inflation was much longer than usual.

NINE

The Control Mechanism

By way of introduction, it is worth observing that the Government's attitude to the buoyant growth of M4 appeared in 1988 to be rather similar to its attitude towards the emergence of the large trade deficit. Chancellor Lawson frequently argued in public that the trade deficit was not a cause for concern because it was the result of behaviour by the private rather than the public sector. If the UK trade deficit had been a reflection of a large *budget* deficit, as in the USA, the Government would have accepted responsibility for taking remedial action. As the cause was private sector behaviour, the Government's policy was one of benign neglect so long as the current account deficit was financed by an inflow of private capital.

In the case of buoyant growth of M4, the Government would have acted if the cause of it had been public sector behaviour—for example, if it had been due to a large PSBR. But it was not. It was a private sector phenomenon; the cause was *the growth of credit*. This was one of the Government's arguments for not taking any action (as long as M0 was not growing too fast).

The reason for the Government's attitude was, presumably, the belief that interference with market forces and individual choice normally does more harm than good. This is, indeed, usually correct. But it should be noted that central banks were founded long before Keynes invented fiscal policy or the huge peace-time growth of the public sector occurred under Labour governments. One reason central banks were thought to be required was because financial systems are not necessarily stable. Financial crises and crashes have been a recurring phenomenon throughout history. They were usually caused by a credit bubble which had been allowed to form and subsequently burst. In 1988 the Treasury may not have thought that the growth of credit in the UK was within its province but it most certainly should have been considered within the sphere of responsibility of the Bank of England.

Demand-side Control

Under the present system of monetary control the UK authorities follow a demand-side rather than a supply-side approach. They

51

consider that the best way of controlling the amount of money in existence is to influence people's demand for it. This is done by varying interest rates. Accordingly, the Bank of England alters interest rates to the level at which the authorities estimate that people's demand for money will fall into line with the target for the money stock. If the authorities get their estimates wrong or if there is an unexpected alteration in one of the other factors influencing the demand for money, for example in the rate of inflation or in the rate of growth of the economy, the money stock will depart from its target path. That is what has been happening.

Under the present mechanism the Bank makes no attempt to control the supply of reserves available to the banking system. The supply is, in effect, without limit. To understand this, it is necessary to appreciate a sequence. The starting point is that a bank can easily persuade one of its customers to issue a commercial bill rather than take a loan; all that is needed is a very slightly lower interest rate. After the commercial bill has been issued, the next step is for it to be 'accepted' (i.e. guaranteed) by the bank and by a discount house. It then becomes a 'primary liquid asset'. The important point is that the total quantity of these primary liquid assets is under the control of banks and not the Bank of England.

The second important feature is that the Bank stands ready in all circumstances either to encash these primary liquid assets or to accept them as collateral for last-resort lending. This is the guarantee of liquidity behind the inter-bank market. It is the reason why bankers can be completely confident that they will always be able to obtain whatever funds they want in that market. The banks' only requirement for balances with the Bank of England is virtually confined to covering errors in the daily forecasts of Exchequer transactions.

To summarise, the supply of primary liquid assets is unlimited and the Bank's willingness to encash them means that the inter-bank market is so liquid that banks have virtually no need for reserves.

Although the Bank of England is prepared to provide banks with liquidity 'in all circumstances', the rate of interest is, of course, not guaranteed. A bank in need of funds may find that it is faced with rising interest rates. In the old days of fixed-rate lending, banks were wary about exposing themselves to a rise in interest rates because they could incur a loss. With the advent of floating-rate lending, banks have passed most of this risk on to their customers. The banks are, therefore, no longer worried about the prospect of rising interest rates. Indeed, if a greater volume of lending means that interest rates will rise, the beneficial effect on profits from the higher volume of business is usually larger than the loss from the rise in interest rates.

Other Constraints

With the Bank willing to provide an unlimited supply of reserves and liquidity, and banks unafraid of a rise in interest rates and wanting to expand their balance sheets, what are the other possible constraints on aggressive selling of loans? One constraint might be a shortage of bank capital, but events during recent years have proved this to be very weak. The enormous loss of capital as a result of LDC debts did not prevent UK banks from tripling their sterling balance sheets between the middle of 1982 and the end of 1988.

There is no doubt that the main constraint under the present system is price control—the Bank, in effect, sets the price which a bank must charge for its product (i.e. for loans). Although bankers compete aggressively with each other to attract new customers and to persuade their existing ones to take out credit lines and arrange overdraft facilities, the amount of these facilities actually used depends on the price—that is, on the rate of interest charged.

If the price mechanism is weak there remains only one constraint, namely, the creditworthiness of borrowers. If the demand for bank loans is not sensitive to a rise in interest rates, as appears to be the case, banks will expand their balance sheets until a significant number of their customers become financially embarrassed. It is important to draw a distinction between isolated cases of a customer becoming financially embarrassed and many customers getting into difficulty at the same time. The first depends on the customer's particular circumstances: bankers have a great deal of practical expertise in assessing such creditworthiness. The second depends on a change in macro-economic conditions, which is outside the particular expertise of most loans officers. There has recently been a very good example of the difference, which is described below.

Personal Collateral

Accurate assessment of the creditworthiness of private individuals is an expensive process. It is much cheaper for a borrower to provide adequate collateral. By far the best form of collateral, and one that is widely available, is a second charge on a borrower's home. As house prices have risen, the market value of many homes has risen well in excess of the main mortgage which was probably taken out when the house was originally purchased. Until the start of the 1980s there were restrictions on the use of this collateral. For years, regulations had discouraged banks and building societies from granting a mortgage on a house for purposes other than the purchase of the house or a home improvement. When the regulations were swept away, people became free to use the collateral for whatever purpose they wanted. For the first time in a long while they became free to get very deeply into debt. But they were not used to this freedom. Very few had experience of the acute pain of taking on too much debt, of having a home repossessed and of being declared bankrupt. As a result, some succumbed to high-pressure salesmanship from financial institutions competing aggressively for business.

From a banker's point of view, the quality of most of the individual loans appeared to be very good since the collateral was excellent. The trouble arose because too many loans were made at the same time. Section 8 described the resulting process of asset price inflation. A classic credit-driven bubble in house prices developed and then burst, at any rate in the South-East of England. As a result of macro-financial forces, therefore, house prices in the South-East have either fallen or are threatening to fall by an amount outside the experience of practical bankers. This means that the collateral may well have fallen below the amount of a loan if the loan was made at a time close to the peak of house prices and if it was for nearly the full amount of the purchase price. *What appeared in micro-terms to be excellent quality lending could turn into quite widespread default.*

TEN

A Bank Loan Versus a Bond Issue

The Alternative of a Bond Issue

As far as a company is concerned, an alternative to borrowing from a bank is to issue a bond. For many years, however, the sterling bond market was virtually dormant except for British government issues. Some people may not be aware of the way in which the market for non-government bonds has reopened in recent years. In 1988 non-British government new issues amounted to no less than £16,500 million. More new money was raised in one year than the British Government ever raised in a single year. The market was also well diversified, consisting of short-, medium- and long-dated bonds, as well as fixed- and variable-rate ones. The re-emergence of a large market is beyond doubt.

Given the capacity of the bond market, UK industrial and commercial companies made surprisingly little use of it. They raised £3,200 million of finance in 1988, which was small compared with their £21,400 million of borrowings from banks. (The main borrowers in the bond market were banks and foreigners.)

The continuing success of banks as financial intermediaries in comparison with the bond market and other financial institutions is particularly remarkable given the changes in comparative advantage during recent years. First, banks now pay interest on many current accounts; they have lost the advantage of not paying interest which they had previously enjoyed under a cartel. Secondly, the prime corporate customers of banks have recently been benefiting from a better credit rating in the market than many banks—that is, they can borrow in the bond market more cheaply than can their bank. Thirdly, the yield curve has often been inverted—that is, short-term interest rates have been above long-term ones and, therefore, the immediate cost of servicing most bank loans has been higher than that for a bond issue. Fourthly, developments in technology, particularly in information and communications, as seen in modern dealing rooms, should have given the bond market a competitive advantage.

What is the reason for the banks' remarkable success? Like other financial institutions, the fundamental role of the banks is to provide a bridge between providers and users of capital. What is the key attraction of the product which banks offer to providers of capital—that is, to savers? And what is the key attraction of the product they offer to users of capital?

Liquidity and Flexibility

The crucial feature which distinguishes a bank deposit from other forms of saving is liquidity. The crucial attribute of a bank loan is flexibility. As far as the latter is concerned, a line of credit from a bank need not be used. When used, the term of a loan can be very flexible. The interest rate can be either floating or fixed, i.e., overnight, seven-day, one-month, three-month, and so on. The currency in which the loan is denominated need not be sterling: it can be dollars, deutschemarks, yen, or whatever.

What is it that enables banks to offer their customers these crucial attributes of liquidity and flexibility? The answer is that they come from the Bank of England, through the way it provides liquidity. There are two aspects which are peculiar to the UK. The first is the degree of provision of liquidity, as described in the previous section. The second is that UK banks pay very little for the services rendered to them by the Bank.

The way most central banks make a charge is either that they do not pay any interest on the reserves which banks keep with them or that they pay a rate below the market one, the size of the charge depending on the amount of reserves and the rate payable. In the USA, for example, the Federal Reserve imposes high mandatory reserve requirements (3 per cent for many types of deposit) on which it does not pay any interest. The banks' loss of interest on these reserves is substantial. Indeed, when interest rates are very high the cost can be excessive, as can be seen from the great difficulty banks have at such times in competing with other financial institutions—for example, with money market mutual funds. In comparison with the Fed's charge in the USA, that made by the Bank of England in the UK is much smaller. In the UK, banks have virtually no need for reserves apart from some very small 'operating deposits', as explained in the previous section. There are, however, additional mandatory reserves but these amount to only one-half per cent of a bank's eligible liabilities. The Bank does not pay any interest on these mandatory reserves but, as they are so small, the loss of interest is also small.

The suggestion is that one of the factors which may have contributed to the growth of bank credit under the UK's present mechanism is that the Bank charges too little for the provision of liquidity and that this gives the banks a competitive advantage over the bond market and other financial institutions.

ELEVEN

Proposal for Change

Financial discipline is fundamental to the control of inflation. Control of the money supply implies a tight constraint on the rate of growth of the balance sheet of the banking sector as a whole. Even more basic is control of the rate of growth of the central bank's own balance sheet. Discipline should start at the top. The Bank of England should limit the growth of its balance sheet.

The Bank holds two main classes of marketable assets, namely bills (either Treasury bills or eligible bills) and foreign exchange. The Bank, like any other bank, has very accurate up-to-date information about its balance sheet. If the Bank's balance sheet is growing too rapidly, it should sell an asset. The Bank could sell either a bill in the domestic money market or foreign currency in the foreign exchange market. In the opposite case, where its balance sheet is growing too slowly, the Bank could buy either a bill or foreign exchange.

The proposal is, therefore, very simple, but the effect is a little more complicated. If the Bank were to control the total of its assets, it would also control the total of its liabilities. Its main liabilities are notes in circulation with the public, banks' vault cash and bankers' deposits. These liabilities comprise 'high-powered money' on which the liquidity of the monetary system ultimately depends. If the Bank were to control the size of its balance sheet, it would control the supply of high-powered money. The control of high-powered money would in turn restrict banks' ability to supply bank deposits, i.e., it would ultimately control the supply of money. The crucial distinction between the proposed system and the present one is that the control would be from the supply-side rather than from the demand-side.

The important operational change under the proposed system would be that the Bank would decide on the size of its daily transactions in the bill and money markets rather than passively allow banks and discount houses to deal in whatever amount they want as at present.

Money Market Operations

The Bank's current operating techniques in the money markets were introduced in August 1981. They were described in 'The Role of the Bank of England in the Money Market' (*Bank of England Quarterly Bulletin*, March 1982). Before discussing them, it is worth making some comments about the Bank's accounts, both those for external publication and those for internal use.

The Bank is legally divided into the Issue Department and the Banking Department and the accounts for external publication are drawn up on this basis. The Issue Department consists of the note issue and the assets which back it. The remaining assets and liabilities are in the Banking Department. The distinction between the two departments is best ignored by laymen as it does not clarify the role of the Bank. Further, the legal holder of the UK's foreign exchange reserves is the Exchange Equalisation Account (EEA). This is a government account and is not part of the Bank; the Bank merely manages the EEA and provides it with day-to-day finance. Again, the distinction between the Bank and the EEA is unhelpful. For many purposes it is best to 'see through' the EEA and assume that the Bank holds the foreign exchange reserves itself.

The internal accounts were described in 'The Management of Money Day by Day' (*Bank of England Quarterly Bulletin*, March 1963). They are divided into three, namely, Exchequer, Bankers and Customers. First, the Bank is the main banker to the government which does not hold balances, other than working amounts, with other banks. Secondly, the Bank is banker to the banking system. Thirdly, foreign central banks are important customers of the Bank (the Bank still retains some commercial banking business but this is best ignored for the purposes of this *Monograph*).

Reverting to the description of the operating techniques introduced in 1981, the following can be derived from the explanation of daily money market operations:

	(i)	The day's increase in the clearing banks' operational balances at the Bank,
plus	(ii)	the rise in the note issue, is equal to
	(iii)	the Exchequer's deficit, i.e. disbursements less receipts,
plus	(iv)	increase in the foreign exchange reserves,
less	(v)	net official sales of central government debt, i.e. of gilt-edged stock, national savings and certificates of tax deposit,
less	(vi)	take up of Treasury bills by the market in accordance with the weekly tender, less maturities in market hands,
plus	(vii)	local authority and commercial bills maturing in the Bank's hands,

plus (viii) 'other' (e.g. transactions by foreign central banks),

less (ix) open-market operations, i.e. sales of bills to the market,

plus (x) increase in lending by the Bank to the market (to discount houses).

The Bank has accurate information at the start of a day about items (iv) to (vii). Gilt-edged transactions, for example, are settled on the business day following the day of execution and the amount of the settlement is, therefore, known at the start of the settlement day. The main doubt is about (iii), that is, about Exchequer disbursements less receipts. The Bank has a reasonable estimate of these, obtained from various government sources, and confirmed in advance in some instances by the receiving or paying banks, but some uncertainties remain and very large swings in the estimate can occur during the day. The picture is not complete until after the conclusion of the day's normal banking business.

There is also doubt about item (viii), 'other'. This includes transactions of foreign central banks. They assist by giving advance notice of likely movements on their accounts where possible, but uncertainty about the total remains.

Advocates of monetary base control argue that items (ix) and (x)—that is, open-market operations and loans to discount houses—could be used to control the equation's total. If the sum of items (iii) to (viii) is known, the Bank could vary items (ix) and (x) to produce the desired result for the total and, hence, for items (i) and (ii)—that is, for banks' balances with the Bank plus the note issue. In this way the Bank could directly control the growth of M0.

As mentioned in the second paragraph of this section, there is also the possibility that the bank could use foreign exchange transactions (item iv) to help control M0.

Buffers

Because the advance information about items (iii) and (viii) is not accurate, some fluctuations in banks' balances with the Bank would occur. The Bank would know the size of the error at the end of the day and could take corrective action the next day or during subsequent days. Certainly, there should be no possibility of a cumulative error building up over time.

Daily fluctuations in banks' balances with the Bank, i.e. in bank reserves, would not be a matter for concern. Far from it; the function of reserves is to act as a buffer. It is important that adequate buffers are built into any system of monetary control. (It should also be noted that short-run fluctuations in the money

60

supply do not matter either. An important role of money is to bridge the gap between the timing of income receipts and expenditure payments. Thus an essential role of money is to act as a buffer. Governments have on occasions appeared to want precise control of the money supply; it would certainly be politically convenient. *Precise control, if it were possible, would in fact be undesirable because money would not then be able to fulfil its essential buffer function. Substitutes would have to be invented.*)[1,2]

---

[1] Some proposals for monetary base control include mandatory reserve ratios for banks. Such ratios normally vary according to the type of deposit, the more liquid the deposit the higher being the ratio. US experience has shown how financial deregulation can lead to changes in type of deposit and, therefore, in the level of required reserves. As a result the distortions which have plagued the monetary aggregates such as M1 (because of NOW accounts, etc.) have also affected the monetary base. This is an important reason why this *Monograph* has not advocated a system of monetary base control which includes mandatory reserve requirements. Another reason is that the flexibility of a non-mandatory system can accommodate variations in the public's preference for notes and coin compared with bank deposits.

[2] The link between open-market operations and control of the Bank's balance sheet requires some elaboration. Money market operations of the sort described would control the assets backing the note issue and banks' balances. The assets which back the other liabilities of the Bank should be excluded from control. The Bank's premises should, for example, be offset against the Bank's capital and reserves; if the Bank were to move to more expensive premises, monetary policy should not be automatically tightened! Further, at the time of the 'bill mountain' in 1985, substantial deposits were needed from the National Loans Fund (a government account) to finance the Bank's huge holding of commercial bills; to allow for this, bill holdings should be calculated net of public sector deposits. Another example is that the foreign exchange reserves should be calculated net of central bank swaps and foreign currency deposits, i.e. net of the Bank's liabilities to foreign central banks.

TWELVE

The Debate

Some History

The Conservatives came to power in May 1979. The argument that monetary policy should be based on a firm foundation raged throughout their first year of office. The Bank's first public response was an article, 'Monetary base control', by Foot, Goodhart and Hotson, in its June 1979 *Quarterly Bulletin*. The Green Paper, *Monetary Control* (Cmnd. 7858), followed in March 1980. Another notable event was a seminar at Church House, Westminster, chaired jointly by Mr Peter Middleton (since knighted and promoted to Permanent Secretary of the Treasury) and Mr John Fforde (executive director of the Bank of England in charge of domestic monetary policy and now retired). The decision was eventually taken at Prime Ministerial level. It was that the old demand-side approach should continue.

There was an attempt to re-open the debate shortly after the Conservatives won a second term of office in June 1983. The important personnel had changed. Mr Nigel Lawson had succeeded Sir Geoffrey Howe as Chancellor of the Exchequer, Mr Robin Leigh-Pemberton was the new Governor of the Bank of England, and, importantly, Mr Eddie George had taken over responsibility for domestic monetary policy from Mr Fforde. Disappointingly, the advocates of a firm foundation lost again. They did so because they could not answer an important practical point. The Bank would inevitably have to be in charge of implementing the change to the new system and the Bank remained implacably hostile.[1]

A Crucial Issue

Looking back on the debate now that sufficient time for reflection has elapsed, it appears to the author that the crucial issue in dispute was whether control over the supply of money would be merely another way of setting interest rates or whether there would

---

[1] See Gordon Pepper, *A Firm Foundation for Monetary Policy*, IEA Inquiry No. 8, IEA, 1989.

be channels of transmission in addition to those operating through interest rates.

There were, indeed, other channels before deregulation occurred. Credit controls meant that banks had to turn away some borrowers, despite their creditworthiness. Building societies also rationed loans when they were short of funds. Some people were either denied credit or had to wait for a loan and thus had to curtail their planned expenditure.

Since deregulation, the money and credit markets have become extremely efficient. It is argued that creditworthy borrowers are no longer denied credit, that there is no rationing, and that any variation in supply is immediately reflected in price (i.e. in interest rates). If markets are truly efficient, it is argued, the whole impact of control over the supply of money would be through variations in interest rates affecting demand.

This argument about the channels of transmission of monetary policy is not confined to discussion of monetary base control. It is one of the basic disagreements between monetarists and Keynesians. Whereas monetarists draw attention to changes in monetary growth when describing macro-economic events, Keynesians focus on changes in interest rates. Keynesians often argue that the monetarist analysis does not add anything to their description of the impact on the economy of changes in interest rates.

Monetary Flows as Distinct from Interest-rate Changes

The following is a simple illustration of the additional information which can come from the behaviour of the money supply. It is included in an attempt to communicate with Keynesians and demand-side analysts.

Market-determined interest rates can rise for three reasons:

o   a rise in inflationary expectations;

o   an increase in the demand for money, generated by overheating of the business cycle; or

o   a decrease in the supply of money, as the effects of tighter monetary policy permeate the economy.

It is extremely important to be able to distinguish the third reason from the first two. If a rise in interest rates is the result of either of the first two, monetary policy is accommodating the increase in inflationary pressure and, therefore, interest rates should be increased further. In contrast, if a rise in interest rates is the result of the third reason, monetary policy is resisting the rise in inflation and, probably, need not be tightened further.

The most important method of distinguishing between the reasons is to examine the behaviour of the money stock. Monetary growth will be excessive if the explanation for the increase in interest rates is either of the first two reasons. Monetary growth will be falling if the explanation is the third reason. This is why it is so important to monitor the behaviour of the money supply as well as to pay attention to interest rates.

Money as a Buffer

Some economists may have trouble with the above description because it implies that the demand for money can differ from its supply. One way of understanding how this can happen is to focus on money's essential role as a buffer bridging the interval of time between expenditure being incurred and income being received. The level of money a person holds is usually different from the ultimately desired balance. It will be larger if income is either higher or has been received sooner than expected, or if expenditure has been delayed or is lower than expected. Conversely, it will be lower if expenditure has occurred sooner than expected or if income has been delayed, etc. The person will subsequently take action to restore his money balance to the desired level. This action may be economic or financial—that is, either expenditure on goods and services can be adjusted or an asset can be bought or sold.

At any point of time many people will be in the process of adjusting their monetary positions towards their desired balance. Some people will be adjusting in one direction whilst others will be adjusting in the opposite direction. On average they can be attempting either to increase or to decrease their balances. Interest rates will be affected as short-term assets are bought or sold, but this will not be the sole effect. Expenditure on long-term assets may also alter but, importantly, expenditure on goods and services will be directly affected.

The Supply of Money and the Behaviour of the Private Sector

Over the last two decades there have been two excellent examples of the way in which excess money can have a direct impact in addition to its impact via interest rates. In the early 1970s M3 was much higher than the economists at the Bank could explain from their equations for the demand for money. These economists were very slow to accept that M3 had departed from its demand schedule and that the reason for the excess was buoyancy of supply. Monetarists argued vehemently at the time that some of the excess supply of money would be spent directly on goods and services and that the outcome would be inflation. Subsequent events provided powerful support for this argument.

The second example was in the 1980s when £M3 and bank lending were again very buoyant. Monetary economists argued, as described in Section 8, that some of the excess money was being spent directly on long-term assets, that this was fuelling the speculation in the stock and property markets at the time, and that a financial bubble was building up. Subsequent events again provided powerful support for the monetarist argument. In particular, similar events occurred in the USA, and the October 1987 crash in the stock market is easy to explain from monetarist theory.

The Supply of Reserves and the Behaviour of Banks

Having illustrated how variations in the supply of money can definitely have important direct effects on the economy at large, which are additional to those operating through interest rates, the argument then is that there would be similar direct effects from variations in the supply of bank reserves.

It must be admitted that one difference between a bank and a private individual would be the speed of response if a balance differed from the desired level. A private individual may be quite content for his balance to move gradually towards the desired level. A bank, in contrast, would probably try to achieve its desired level of reserves on a daily basis. The main way of attempting to do so would be by carrying out transactions in the inter-bank market. If a bank had surplus reserves, for example, the simplest course of action would be for it not to roll-over borrowing from other banks. If no loans were maturing, surplus funds could be deposited in the market. Inter-bank rates of interest would be affected and this would influence other rates of interest. The monetarist argument is that there would also be other important effects.

The transactions in the inter-bank market would merely pass the surplus reserves from one bank to another. It would be like a game of 'pass the parcel'. At the close of business, the surplus would remain somewhere in the system. The commercial banks would not be able to destroy reserves because their total volume would be under the sole control of the Bank. The way in which equilibrium could be restored would be for banks either to acquire investments from the non-bank private sector (because the Bank would not, under monetary base control, be prepared to supply them) or to increase their loans. Both types of transaction would increase the money supply and, therefore, banks' demand for reserves. Equilibrium would be reached by the demand for reserves rising into line with supply.

Holdings of gilt-edged stock are a good example of an investment by banks. The argument is that a bank with surplus reserves would be more likely to purchase gilt-edged stock than a bank with inadequate reserves. Any stockbroker or bond salesman is well aware that a client with surplus funds is much more likely to respond to an offer of stock than one who is short of funds. The price must, of course, be right. If it is, the volume of business from an institution which is flush with funds will be much greater than that from an institution which is short of funds. The crucial factor is not solely price but the combination of price and availability of funds.

The explanation for price not being the sole factor is largely decision-taking inertia. With the benefit of hindsight, investment decisions often appear to have been abundantly obvious and, therefore, to have been easy to take. At the time when a decision has to be taken, in contrast, the uncertainties nearly always appear to be great and the decision requires effort. There is no doubt that the easy option is to do nothing. When an institution has surplus funds, the decision-taking inertia is broken by the existence of the surplus, which has to be invested somewhere. An institution with surplus funds is, accordingly, much more likely to respond positively to an offer of stock than one which is short of funds.

The point about decision-taking inertia is very important. It is not about laziness. Investment managers are only too well aware how difficult it is to out-perform a market and that the outturn will most probably be that successful transactions will be almost exactly balanced by unsuccessful ones. Many investment managers take the view that their chance of overall success will be increased if they confine their transactions to ones about which they are reasonably confident at the time. If they are not reasonably confident, they do not act unless they either have money to invest or need to disinvest.

The way people react to news is also important. If an unexpected item of good news occurs, people will purchase more stock when they have surplus funds waiting to be invested than when they are short of funds. If an unexpected item of bad news occurs, people will sell more stock when they are short of funds than when they have surplus funds. The combination of unexpected news and cash position breaks the decision-taking inertia.

Conclusion

The conclusion is that the decision-taking inertia which exists in practice means that markets are not 'perfect'. Under a régime of monetary base control a bank with surplus funds would be more likely to purchase gilt-edged stock than one which was short of funds. This is highly relevant because purchases of stock from the non-bank private sector by banks boosts the money supply in the same way as purchases by the Bank. The availability of bank reserves would have effects other than those operating through changes in rates of interest in the inter-bank market. Control of bank reserves would not be merely another way of setting interest rates. Variations in the supply of surplus bank reserves would have a direct impact on the money supply and therefore on the economy.

Appendix to Section Twelve

Speed of Response of Demand and Supply

Consider first, a market for a commodity in which either the supply or the demand responds quickly to a change in price. Suppose that supply and demand are equal at the current price but that the one or the other subsequently alters. The price will rapidly change to a new level at which supply and demand will again be equalised. Everyone who wishes to buy or sell at the new price will be able to do so. In technical language, the market will clear.

Contrast this with the market for a second commodity for which neither the supply nor the demand responds quickly to a change in price. Suppose that the market for this second commodity is in equilibrium at the current price but that subsequently either supply or demand alters. The market will not clear again at once. If demand has increased, the price will rise but this will not quickly encourage additional supply, or discourage the increase in demand unless the rise in price is extreme. Stocks will fall and someone who wishes to buy at the ruling price may be told by a supplier that stocks have run out—that is to say, the buyer must wait for a new delivery. If supply has increased, the price will fall but this will not quickly encourage additional demand or discourage the increase in supply and stocks will rise.

Suppose that the authorities wish to control the total amount of the second type of commodity in existence. They can try to do so by controlling either supply or demand. They can, first, attempt to control demand by continuously varying the price, but the quantity will behave erratically because demand responds only slowly to price changes. If the authorities persist with the policy, the quantity will eventually be controlled but the fluctuations in the commodity's price may be large, especially if the supply alters unexpectedly because of a non-price factor.

The second way for the authorities to control the quantity of the second type of commodity is to control its supply. The total of the commodity in existence will be far more stable than under the first method. This does not imply suppression of the price mechanism. The price will fluctuate as demand changes. However, as erratic fluctuations in supply will be controlled at source, fluctuations in price because of unexpected variations in supply will not occur and the resulting ones may well be smaller than if control were via demand, especially if adequate stocks are held. This suggests strongly that control of supply is more efficient than control of demand if a commodity is of the second type.

Money is clearly a commodity of the second type. Neither the demand nor the supply of money responds quickly to changes in its price, i.e. to a change in interest rates. The efficient method of controlling the amount of money in existence is, therefore, control of supply rather than control of demand.

THIRTEEN

The Exchange Rate Mechanism of the European Economic Community

An important reason why Chancellor Lawson decided to shadow the deutschemark in 1987 may well have been that he had lost confidence in the UK's domestic mechanism for monetary control and, rather than reform it, he chose the external option. It must be emphasised, however, that the need to reform the domestic mechanism would not be avoided merely by the UK joining the Exchange Rate Mechanism (ERM) of the European Monetary System (EMS). There are the following variations within ERM:

(i)   A continuation of the present régime of intervention in foreign exchange markets and occasional changes in parities.

(ii) A continuation of the present régime but with the UK following a policy of not 'sterilising' any foreign exchange outflow or inflow. Intervention in the foreign exchange market is said to be sterilised if its impact on the money supply is offset by official operations in the gilt-edged market. A policy of refraining from sterilisation would mean that intervention in the foreign exchange market to stop sterling from falling below its band would reduce the money supply—that is, monetary policy would automatically be tightened. The discipline would be similar to that of the pre-1914 Gold Standard. (Another régime which would be very similar would be for the Bank of England to operate as a Currency Board which was subsidiary to the Bundesbank.)

(iii) Currencies competing with each other within ERM.

(iv) An early move to a European common currency.

(v)   A breakdown of the system of fixed exchange rates, that is, ERM not leading to a common currency.

Under (ii) and (iv) above, there would be no need for the UK to reform its domestic mechanism for monetary control; under (i), (iii) and (v) the need would remain, as explained below.

Continuation of the Present Régime

Under the present ERM régime, countries must harmonise their domestic monetary policies if massive intervention in foreign exchange markets is to be avoided. A country's ability to control the stance of its monetary policy continues to be very important. The need for the UK to reform its domestic mechanism would therefore remain.

Competing Currencies

There are powerful arguments for a gradual introduction of a European common currency. Many people think that fixed exchange rates are an intermediate stage between floating rates and a common currency. *This is wrong*, as has been explained repeatedly by Milton Friedman:

'The basic fact is that a unified currency and a system of freely floating exchange rates are members of the same species even though superficially they appear very different. Both are free market mechanisms for interregional or international payments. Both permit exchange rates to move freely. Both exclude any administrative or political intermediary in payments between residents of different areas. Either is consistent with free trade between areas, or with a lessening of trade restrictions.

'On the other hand, national currencies linked by pegged exchange rates, whether or not through the mechanism of gold, and a system of variable exchange rates, controlled and manipulated by governmental bodies, either through an adjustable peg or day-to-day market operations, are also members of the same species. Both are interventionist standards. Neither, in my opinion, is consistent with a permanent lessening of barriers to international trade, but only with oscillating barriers as nations shift from surplus to deficit.'[1]

There is a substantial amount of analysis[2] which shows that there is only one way to move gradually and successfully towards a European common currency and that is to allow currencies to float and compete with each other during an interim period. A system could be designed so that good money would drive out bad. The best money would be the winner. The common currency would materialise as the best money defeated the others. Further, and most importantly, the process would ensure that the common

---

[1] Milton Friedman, 'Should There Be an Independent Monetary Authority?', in Leland B. Yeager (ed.), *In Search of a Monetary Constitution*, Cambridge, Mass.: Harvard University Press, 1962, reprinted in *Dollars and Deficits, Inflation, Monetary Policy and the Balance of Payments*, Englewood Cliffs: Prentice-Hall, 1968, pp. 173-94, and, similarly, in the *Financial Times*, 18 December 1989.

[2] Roland Vaubel, *Choice in European Monetary Union*, Occasional Paper 55, IEA, 1979; Geoffrey E. Wood, 'Banking and Monetary Control after 1992—A Central Bank for Europe?', in *Whose Europe?*, IEA Readings No. 29, IEA, 1989.

currency was soundly based; currency reform would be ensured throughout Europe.

If the competing currency proposal is adopted, reform of the domestic mechanism of control in the UK would be most urgent. Anyone who has studied the history of monetary policy in the UK in the 1980s and who has read the description of the present mechanism of monetary control should have very little doubt that sterling would have no chance of competing against the deutschemark—the Bank of England would not have any hope in a contest with the Bundesbank—if the present mechanism of monetary control is retained.

Breakdown of ERM

There are many examples in economics of intervention in markets, by very able people who have the best of intentions, which has precisely the opposite effect in the longer term to that intended. There is a highly reputable school of thought which is convinced that the ERM system of fixed exchange rates is intervention of this type. Some of the economists who are the most enthusiastic about a common currency are the most hostile to ERM. If they are correct, ERM will break down and, after it has done so, reform of the domestic mechanism of monetary control in the UK will be essential.

FOURTEEN

Summary

Behaviour of M0

o Prior to October 1987 (the stock market crash) interest rates were raised within a month or so of whenever M0's three-month rate of growth exceeded the target range for the fiscal year as a whole.

o On every occasion M0's growth subsequently fell back within its target range.

o On the eve of the stock market crash M0's excessive rate of growth had persisted despite a 1 per cent rise in base rates in August 1987. After the crash, interest rates were altered in the wrong direction to correct the behaviour of M0. The excessive growth continued until the end of December.

o After a two-month lull, M0's growth rebounded upwards in March 1988. For a second time interest rates were moved in the wrong direction (during the attempt to shadow the deutsche-mark). The result was that excessive monetary growth gathered considerable momentum.

Assessment

o M0's track record as a coincidental indicator of inflationary pressure has been good.

o It should be emphasised that M0 is more of a *coincidental* than a leading indicator of inflationary pressure.

o The present mechanism of control over M0 is weak. Interest rates have very little direct impact. The mechanism is the indirect one of an increase in interest rates affecting first the economy in general and retail sales in particular, and then the demand for notes and coin. Interest rates may not have a powerful impact unless they are raised by a sufficient amount to shock confidence.

o   If control is to be achieved over a reasonably short period, the mechanism may be adequate to correct only minor departures of M0 from the desired path. It is, therefore, important that corrective action is taken promptly, probably as soon as growth during the latest three months has departed from the target range for the year as a whole, providing allowance has been made for known special factors.

o   Because the control mechanism is weak, the authorities cannot afford to wait, as they should be able to, to find out if a departure of M0 from its desired path is merely a fluctuation which will reverse of its own accord in due course.

o   The conclusion is that, if M0 is to be the key target variable, its control mechanism should definitely be strengthened.

Foreign Exchange Rate

o   Prior to the Louvre Accord in 1987, there was downward pressure on sterling, seen most clearly from the foreign exchange reserves, on every occasion that buoyant growth of M0 gave cause for concern.

o   After the start of the massive intervention in the foreign exchange market in 1987, supposedly under the Louvre Accord but in practice to peg sterling to the deutschemark, the sterling exchange rate was at first a badly misleading and then a very late indicator of inflationary pressure.

Broad Money—M3 or M4

o   Broad money can be a very misleading indicator on some occasions.

o   Broad money has two components, namely, money held for transactions purposes and money held for savings purposes. Variations in demand for the latter are an important explanation for broad money being misleading.

o   Indications that broad money may be misleading are, first, contrary behaviour of the narrower monetary aggregates dominated by transactions money and, second, marked changes in the merits of bank and building society deposits as an investment *vis-à-vis* other savings media—that is, large changes in relative interest rates.

o   That broad money is a misleading indicator on some occasions does not mean that it is not of value for much of the time.

Causes of Monetary Growth

o   If the Bank of England controlled the quantity of bank reserves, causality would run from bank reserves to money and from money to GDP. Analysis could then start with the behaviour of bank reserves.

o   The Bank does not act in this way. Analysis should, therefore, start a stage earlier, with the reasons for the current behaviour of the money supply.

o   Lending by banks and building societies was an extremely important reason for excessive monetary growth in recent years.

o   The direct impact of fiscal policy was of minor importance. This is true whether the stance of fiscal policy is measured by the PSBR or by the size of tax cuts. The cut in taxation in the 1988 Budget did, however, have an indirect effect because it boosted confidence and thus made people more willing to borrow.

o   Foreign exchange intervention also had little direct impact, because it was completely sterilised. As with fiscal policy, there was an indirect effect but, more importantly, foreign exchange intervention diverted attention from the behaviour of the money supply at a crucial time.

o   Debt policy was not a cause of excessive monetary growth. It was a powerful weapon which could have been used to mop up excessive growth from time to time, but it was neglected.

o   The policy of generally not overfunding should not have meant that aggressive debt sales were ruled out over short periods, as a temporary expedient.

Control of Credit

o   Control of credit is one of the basic functions of a central bank; it is the responsibility of the Bank of England rather than the Treasury.

o   Banks continue to be extraordinarily successful compared with other financial intermediaries.

o   The crucial attributes offered by banks are liquidity for savers and flexibility for borrowers.

o   These attributes flow from the Bank of England which charges much less for the provision of the service than does the Federal Reserve in the USA.

o The smallness of the charge gives banks a competitive advantage over other financial intermediaries in the UK.

o With the Bank of England an unlimited provider of reserves and liquidity and with banks having access to capital, there are only two constraints on aggressive selling of loans: first, the rate of interest charged for the product is set by the Bank and, secondly, the creditworthiness of borrowers.

o As the demand for loans is not sensitive to changes in interest rates, expansions of credit may tend to continue until there is a widespread danger of default.

The Proposals

o Financial discipline is fundamental to the control of inflation. Control of the money supply implies a tight constraint on the rate of growth of the balance sheet of the banking sector as a whole. Even more basic is control of the rate of growth of the central bank's own balance sheet. Discipline should start at the top. The Bank of England should limit the growth of its balance sheet.

o The Bank can control the growth of its balance sheet by buying or selling assets, either bills in the domestic money markets or foreign currency in the foreign exchange market.

o Monetary control would be from the supply-side rather than from the demand-side.

o The important operational change under the proposed system would be that the Bank would decide on the size of its daily transactions in the bill and money markets rather than passively allow banks and discount houses to deal in whatever amount they wanted as at present.

The Debate

o Keynesians and demand-side analysts dispute whether an excess supply of money or of bank reserves can have an effect on the economy other than that operating through changes in interest rates.

o During the last two decades there have been two excellent examples of the supply of money differing from the demand for it and of effects occurring other than those operating through interest rates: in the early 1970s excess supply was spent directly on goods and services which led to product price inflation; in the 1980s excess supply was spent directly on long-term assets which led to a boom in the stock and housing markets—that is, to asset price inflation.

o Differences between the supply and demand for bank reserves would similarly have direct effects.

The Exchange Rate Mechanism

o An important reason why Chancellor Lawson decided to shadow the deutschemark in 1987 may well have been that he had lost confidence in the UK's domestic mechanism for monetary control; rather than reform it, he chose the external option.

o The need to reform the domestic monetary mechanism would not be avoided merely by the UK joining the Exchange Rate Mechanism (ERM) of the European Monetary System (EMS).

o It would be avoided if the UK followed a policy of not 'sterilising' any foreign exchange outflow or inflow. The discipline would then be similar to the pre-1914 Gold Standard.

o It would also be avoided if ERM led quickly to a European common currency.

o Reform of the domestic monetary mechanism would continue to be necessary if there were merely a continuation of the present ERM régime of intervention in foreign exchange markets and occasional changes in parities.

o Reform would become most urgent if the proposal to allow currencies to compete with each other within the ERM were adopted. Sterling would have no chance of competing against the deutschemark—the Bank would not have any hope in a contest with the Bundesbank—if the present mechanism of monetary control in the UK were to be retained.

o If the ERM system of fixed exchange rates breaks down, reform of the domestic mechanism of monetary control in the UK would become essential.

FIFTEEN

Policy Conclusion

The policy conclusion is very simple. The Bank of England should be instructed to control the growth of its balance sheet. The rate of growth should be agreed each year with the Government and reported to Parliament. Any significant departure should be reported both to the Government and to the Finance Committee of the House of Commons, the onus of proof remaining wholly with the Bank to justify the departure.

Select Bibliography

Bank of England, *Quarterly Bulletin:*

'Operation of monetary policy', quarterly commentaries.

J. S. Fforde, 'Setting monetary objectives', June 1983.

M. D. K. W. Foot, C. A. E. Goodhart, and L. A. C. Hotson, 'Monetary base control', June 1979.

'Financial change and broad money', speech by the Governor, December 1986.

HM Treasury, *Monetary Control*, Cmnd. 7858, London: HMSO, 1980.

Cagan, Philip, 'The uncertain future of monetary policy', in F. Capie and G. E. Wood (eds.), *Monetary Economics in the 1980s*, London: Macmillan, 1989.

Congdon, Tim, *Monetarism Lost*, London: Centre for Policy Studies, 1989.

Friedman, Milton, 'Should There Be an Independent Monetary Authority?', in M. Friedman (ed.), *Dollars and Deficits, Inflation, Monetary Policy and the Balance of Payments*, Englewood Cliffs, New Jersey: Prentice-Hall Inc., 1968.

Johnston, R. B., 'The demand for non-interest bearing money in the UK', Treasury Working Paper No. 28, 1984.

Lawson, Nigel, Lombard Association Speech, HM Treasury, 1986.

————, Mais Lecture, HMT, 1984.

————, Mansion House Speeches, HMT, 1983, 1985 and 1989.

Pepper, Gordon, *A firm foundation for monetary policy*, IEA Inquiry No. 8, London: Institute of Economic Affairs, 1989.

Walters, Alan, *Britain's Economic Renaissance*, Oxford: Oxford University Press, 1986.

————, *Sterling and Inflation in the Eighties*, Collins/IEA, (forthcoming).

Wood, Geoffrey E., 'Banking and Monetary Control after 1992—A Central Bank for Europe?', in *Whose Europe?*, Readings No. 29, IEA, 1989.

Vaubel, Roland, *Choice in European Monetary Union*, Occasional Paper 55, IEA, 1979.